Ma

Delaplaine 2019

THE

LONG WEEKEND GUIDE

Andrew Delaplaine

NO BUSINESS HAS PAID A SINGLE PENNY OR GIVEN <u>ANYTHING</u> TO BE INCLUDED IN THIS BOOK.

A list of the author's other travel guides, as well as his political thrillers and titles for children, can be found at the end of this book.

Senior Editors – **Renee & Sophie Delaplaine**
Senior Writer – **James Cubby**
Art Director – **Chip McGoldrick**

Gramercy Park Press
New York – London – Paris

Please submit corrections, additions or comments to
andrewdelaplaine@mac.com

MARSEILLE
The Delaplaine
Long Weekend Guide

TABLE OF CONTENTS

Chapter 1
WHY MARSEILLE?

It's so hard to begin when it comes to listing the great attributes of this truly unique city on the sea.

It's the oldest city in France, settled in ancient times by the Greeks. Marseille was already 500 years old when Caesar appeared at the city walls to lay siege in 49 B.C.

More recently, in the 20th Century, when immigrants from Algeria and other colonials from the remnant of the French Empire overseas started to swarm here, the city became quite unique in France because it was so culturally, psychologically and ethnically different from the rest of the country. Crime also soared as the city took on an image of grittiness and danger. But for all its ups and downs—and it's had plenty of both—Marseille has nonetheless remained a world-class city.

And while it's the biggest port in France (and the fifth largest in Europe), you still can see fishermen bring in their daily catch, an image that's as profound as any in all of Provence. The subtext to this amazing juxtaposition of old and new: It's all about the food.

The French national anthem, La Marseillaise, which we all remember from the movie "Casablanca," was written and composed by Claude Joseph Rouget de Lisle in 1792. The French National Convention adopted it as the Republic's anthem in 1795. The name of the song comes from the fact that it was first sung on the streets by volunteers from Marseille.

Because of its location, Marseille has for thousands of years been a crossroads where cultures combine (sometimes the word "combust" would seem more appropriate). This has given Marseille over the years a justified reputation for rough edges, for danger, for colorful characters, for a heady mix of internationalism, for crime. Many French themselves steer away from the teeming city, preferring the more sedate environs of nearby Avignon, Arles, Nîmes or Aix-en-Provence, none of them approaching the level of excitement or cosmopolitanism you get here in Marseille.

If you want to read a couple of excellent books around Marseille, read **M.F.K. Fisher's** "Consider the Oyster" or "The Gastronomical Me," when she, a naïve California girl, moved with her husband to Dijon before World War II. I love all her books. She captures the scruffiness of Marseille, the edginess of it, the *danger* of it.

When the European Union named Marseille a European Capital of Culture in 2013, an intense light shone on Marseille, giving it a more visible profile. And yes, the city has spruced itself up, added a new wardrobe, invigorated numerous new cultural institutions, opened new attractions, rehabbed hundreds of old warehouses into arts centers.

By the 12th Century Fort St.-Jean you'll cross a little bridge that leads you into the historic district of **Le Panier** (which translates as "the Basket"). This is where immigrants have long settled when they moved into Marseille from Italy or Corsica or Sicily or Turkey. Now it's home to an increasing number of artists. It's very hilly and made a perfect place for Resistance fighters to hide during World War II, so much so that the Nazis blew up parts of it.

The **Vieille Charité** is the center of the historic district. Here you'll find museums dedicated to exhibits of Mediterranean archaeology and African, Oceanic and American Indian art. The only way to absorb this part of town is to walk through it— through the narrowest streets and alleys lined on one side and the other with cafes, stores, workshops, artists' havens, fashionable lofts where you'd like to move tomorrow. The **Place des Moulins** at the top of the hill is where, shaded by trees, you'll find a square from which you can see miles out to sea. Artillery once stood here, forming a battery where they could shoot at approaching enemy ships.

If you go back down to Ft.-St. Jean, you'll see another bridge that leads you to a wide plaza, or esplanade, where the crowning jewel of Marseille's rebirth can be found, the new **Musée des Civilisations de l'Europe et de la Méditerranée (MuCEM)**, designed by Rudy Ricciotti. (Interestingly, MuCEM is the first national museum ever designated outside Paris.) Also here is the Stefano Boeri-designed **Villa Méditerranée**. These two stunning museums were paid for with funds that came with the European Union designation. The money was well spent, let me tell you. From this vantage point you can see wide-ranging views of the city, all the way from the statue of **Notre-Dame de la Garde** on the south to the commanding **Cathédrale de la Major** on the north side.

It's well worth noting that the restaurants within MuCEM are run by **Chef Gerald Passédat,** who holds 3 Michelin stars.

Though these foods will be hard to avoid while visiting Marseille, I'm pointing them out here so that you know I want you to be certain to try them all because wherever in the world you travel, you won't get these dishes prepared any better than here in Marseille:

Aioli is a Provençal traditional sauce made of garlic, olive oil, lemon juice and egg yolks. There are many variations, but they're all good (to me, anyway). Just eat it with olives and you've got a treat.

Tapenade, a dish made of finely chopped or puréed olives, capers, anchovies and olive oil. Simply spread it on a crusty piece of bread and you're in heaven.

Bouillabaisse, that wonderful fresh fish soup from the sea, is so reminiscent of Marseille that I always think of the city whenever I order it elsewhere in the world. (And, like I said, it's almost never as good as they make it here.) Bouillabaisse has an interesting history. It originally was a stew made by Marseille fishermen using the bony rockfish restaurants and markets wouldn't buy from them. So they were stuck with it and had to make do. They tossed in vegetables, mussels, other shellfish, added different fish like bream, sea robin, monkfish, pretty much whatever was available. The result is a spectacularly flavorful stew you'll never forget (and find difficult to replicate).

Pastis. This is the drink of Provence. It's an anise-flavored liqueur and aperitif, usually 40% to 45% alcohol. I drink it day and night when I'm here. (It will kick your ass if you're not careful.)

After the important European Union designation, people have started to notice this city of less than 900,000. To see it in a new light, through a new perspective. And now they see what a truly fabulous place it is.

Funny thing, but Fisher knew it all those years ago when she swallowed the briny oysters she first found here, in wonderfully alive Marseille.

Chapter 2
GETTING ABOUT

The Public Transportation, also known as "**RTM**," offers a system of buses covering the city with 90 lines. The metro on the other hand has 2 lines only but 28 stops. The new tram system is a great service. You can count on making great use of it.

All services operate daily from 5 a.m. to 1 a.m. Cost is a couple of euros.

Check out the **City Pass** – this bargain allows you to get around the city cheaply. Information at the tourism site just below.

There is also a very convenient water shuttle from the Old Port.

The city offers a free bike service monitored with a tracking system from 6am to 12am daily with 130 stations.

Chapter 3
WHERE TO STAY

AU VIEUX PANIER

13, rue du Panier, Marseille, 4-91-91-23-72
NEIGHBORHOOD: Hotel de Ville, Les Grandes
Carmes
www.auvieuxpanier.com
This is a most unusual B&B in that it started out as
a 17th Century Corsican grocer's shop. The 5 rooms
were all decorated (each quite differently) by local
artists. One, by Julien Colombier, is dark and sexy.
Another, by Thomas Canto, is sleek and modern.
One has slabs of wood hanging from the ceiling. The

public areas exhibit even more art on a rotating basis. In the middle of the historic old town.

BASTIDE DE CAPELONGUE
Les Claparèdes, Chemin des Cabanes, Bonnieux, +33 4 90 75 89 78
www.capelongue.com/en
NEIGHBORHOOD: Luberon.
Located in a rustic stone building, this upscale hotel offers 17 beautiful rooms – each carrying the name of a famous character from literature of Provence. Amenities include: Free Wi-Fi, flat-screen TVs, and balconies (in some of the rooms). Facilities include: 2 restaurants with patio dining, an outdoor pool, gardens with sitting areas and a playground.

C2 HOTEL
48 Rue Roux de Brignoles, Marseille, +33 4 95 05 13 13
www.c2-hotel.com
NEIGHBORHOOD: Palais de Justice area
One thing you could never find in Marseille was the kind of "boutique" hotel you could find in almost any city anywhere. That has changed recently, like the C2 for example. Formerly a private 19th century mansion, this hotel features 20 spacious rooms. Amenities include: free Wi-Fi and flat-screen TVs. Hotel features include: spa with indoor pool and Jacuzzi, a bar, and a beach. You get to the beach by taking a 15-minute boat ride to their little island, Ile Degaby. Non-smoking hotel.

CASA HONORE
123, rue Sainte, Marseille, 33-4-91-33-08-34
NEIGHBORHOOD: Saint Victor
www.casahonore.com
This B&B was a printing plant before it was
converted into 4 lovely rooms. They are small, but
clean and modern. Marseille has 300 days of sunshine
each year, and all that suns keeps the courtyard with
its nice landscaping lush all year. Breakfast served
in morning from 7. The lobby has cushy white seats
and a huge wooden coffee table overlooking the yard,
where there's also a swimming pool. Very cozy.

CHATEAU SAINT-MARTIN & SPA
2490 Avenue des Templiers, Vence, +33 4 93 58 02 02
www.chateau-st-martin.com
NEIGHBORHOOD: Vence
This luxury seasonal hotel offers plush rooms
and beautiful views. If you enjoy sumptuous
appointments, you'll love the gilt-edged mirrors,

parquet floors and tapestries you'll find when you walk into this place. Amenities include: Free Wi-Fi and flat-screen TVs. Hotel features include: marble bathrooms, balconies and terraces, an oak-paneled bar, a fine-dining restaurant, an outdoor grill, a spa, a pool, tennis courts, and access to a private beach.

HOTEL CRILLON LE BRAVE

Place de l'Eglise, Crillon-le-Brave, +33 4 90 65 61 61
www.crillonlebrave.com
NEIGHBORHOOD: Provence
This hotel includes several 17th & 18th century buildings with 28 double bedrooms in several sizes and 7 suites. Amenities include: free Wi-Fi, CD & DVD library, mini-bar and safe, DVD and flat screen satellite TVs. Facilities include: Pool, restaurant, bar, lounge and spa. Pet Friendly. Non-smoking rooms available.

HOTEL LA RESIDENCE
18, Quai du Port, Marseille, 4-91-91-91-22
NEIGHBORHOOD: Hotel de Ville
www.hotel-residence-marseille.com
Has commanding view of the harbor. Be sure to get
a room with one of these great views. (Most rooms
have this view, but make sure.) It'll be a big memory
of your trip. This 40-room property was recently
redesigned in a style reminiscent of Le Corbusier,
very 1950s retro chic. You'll love the juxtaposition
of the modern whimsical interior design here in the
Old Port.

HOSTELLERIE LES REMPARTS
72 Rue Grande, Saint-Paul-de-Vence,
+33 4 93 24 06 40
www.hostellerielesremparts.com
NEIGHBORHOOD: Saint-Paul-de-Vence
If you're on a budget, you'll definitely want to stay
here in this house dating back to the 17th Century. It's

located in the heart of the medieval village, this basic B&B offers 9 traditionally furnished rooms right on the old ranmparts. Amenities include: Free Wi-Fi and air conditioning. On-site restaurant serving traditional Provencal cuisine.

INTERCONTINENTAL MARSEILLE
HOTEL DIEU
1 Place Daviel, Marseilles, 4-13-42-42-42
www.intercontinental.com
It may say Intercontinental on the building, but what's interesting here is the building that it's located in. It's a majestic 18th Century structure protected by a historic designation. It overlooks the Old Port and thus offers a panoramic view from its wide terrace. Next to the oldest part of Marseille, known as the Panier. Has all the amenities you'd expect at an Intercontinental: business center, courier service, email & Internet, concierge, secretarial service, extensive fitness center with spectacular floor to

ceiling windows. There's a **Spa by Clarins** offering an indoor pool, 2 saunas and a hammam, 6 treatment booths. Also on site are **Les Fenêtres**, a brasserie, and the more upmarket **L'Alcyone**. Both menus feature local favorites of Provence.

L'OUSTALET
1476 Chemin des Marres, Simiane-Collongue,
+33 6 49 76 53 55
www.loustalet-des-marres.com/en
NEIGHBORHOOD: La Bouilladisse
Beautiful B&B with 3 charming guestrooms. Designed for the traveler seeking an intimate, relaxing experience. Amenities include: Free Wi-Fi, free breakfast, flat-screen TVs with satellite channels and free parking on-site. Facilities include: seating areas, table tennis, and seasonal outdoor pool. Pet-friendly.

LA MAISON DOMAINE DE BOURNISSAC
Montée d'Eyragues, Paluds de Noves,
+33 4 90 90 25 25
www.lamaison-a-bournissac.com
NEIGHBORHOOD: Provence
Set in a 15th-century traditional farmhouse, this hotel offers 13 guestrooms and suites – all decorated differently. Amenities include: Free Wi-Fi, satellite TV, and unique features like marble bathrooms and exposed-stone walls. On-site Mediterranean restaurant with a terrace offering beautiful mountain views, outdoor pool, and sunny terrace. Ideal for a relaxing getaway.

LE COUVENT
HOTEL DE VILLE
6 rue Fonderie Vieille, Marseille, +33 6 12 31 48 79
www.fonderievieille.com
NEIGHBORHOOD: Frankrike

This restored 17th Century convent offers 9 luxury suites complete with kitchen, Wi-Fi, TVs, and all the essentials. A favorite for visiting actors and artists. Conveniently located behind the Old Port, alongside the Place de Lenche, near the Museum of La vieille Charité and the MUCEM. Non-smoking venue. Pets not allowed.

LE CORBUSIER
280, Blvd Michelet, Marseille, 4-28-331-39-22
NEIGHBORHOOD: Sainte Anne
www.hotellecorbusier.com

Well known property a little out of the center of things, and that's why people cherish it. Not to mention that it was designed by the famed architect. The rooms here are decorated in a very Spartan manner, but they are comfortable and each room has a private terrace.

LE PETIT NICE PASSEDAT
17, rue des Braves, Marseille, +33 4 91 59 25 92
NEIGHBORHOOD: Endoume
www.passedat.fr

One of Marseille's most exclusive hotels. It was made by combining 2 villas. It's run by Gérald Passédat, who took over from his dad, Jean-Paul, and whose grandmother was famous opera singer. Boasts 3 Michelin stars. You'll definitely want to dine here even if you don't stay here. The rooms are over-the-top modern and very luxurious.

LES BORIES HOTEL & SPA

Route de Senanque, Gordes, +33 4 90 72 00 51
www.hotellesbories.com
NEIGHBORHOOD: Luberon
Set on 20 acres, this sophisticated spa hotel offers 34
beautifully decorated rooms and suites. Amenities
include: Free Wi-Fi, flat-screen TVs, and mini-
bars. Hotel facilities include: spa features a menu of
treatments, sauna, gym, a French restaurant, beautiful
gardens, tennis court, indoor and outdoor pool, and
guest lounge with a bar.

MGALLERY GRAND HOTEL BEAUVAU

4, rue Beauvau, Marseilles, 4- 91-54-91-00
www.mgallery.com/Marseilles
This Hotel is part of the famous Group "Accor." A
four star recently renovated. Cozy and very quiet.
Right in the heart of the old town, the color scheme
is consistent with the colors of Provence. The interior
is designed along the lines of Louis Philippe and
Napoleon III. Legendary writers and musicians have
stayed in this charming hotel, people like George
Sand, Lamartine and Mérimée to Frédéric Chopin
and Paganini. The rue Beauvau where this hotel is
situated, is one of the oldest streets in all Marseille,
as busy today as it ever has been. Try to get a room
overlooking the Old Port.

MAMA SHELTER MARSEILLE

64, rue de la Loubiere, Marseille, 4-84-35-20-00
www.mamashelter.com
NEIGHBORHOOD: Cours Julien; Notre-Dame-du-Mont

I don't know what it is, but the ubiquitous Philippe Starck seems to have the magic touch of turning whatever property he designs into a trendy spot from the very moment it opens. (I wonder if Ian Schrager, who gave him such a high profile boost when he worked on Schrager's New York hotels and then the Delano in South Beach, gets a commission—he ought to, as he's made Starck very rich.) What Schrager did was create the kind of fashionable hotel property that brought locals into the hotel, not just visitors. Thus, you get a heady mix of great people from in and out of town. This place is no different. And it's not in the most visible of locations. Still, people flock here like bees to honey. The restaurant here, by Chef Alain Senderens, is also a hot hangout. (The hotel reasonably priced, believe it or not, and near 3 Metro stops.)

SOFITEL MARSEILLE VIEUX PORT

36, Blvd Charles Livon, Marseille, 4-91-15-59-00
NEIGHBORHOOD: Le Pharo
www.sofitel-marseille-vieuxport.com
Upmarket hotel with lots of luxury and superior views
of the Old Port. The fancy bar here is very popular.
They even give pets a water bowl, or, if you like, a
meal prepared for the dogs.

VILLA MARIE JEANNE

4 Rue Chicot, Marseille, +33 4 91 85 51 31
www.villa-marie-jeanne.com
NEIGHBORHOOD: Saint Barnabé

An 18th century stone manor house transformed into a wonderful Bed & Breakfast that offers 3 charming rooms, and 2 apartments. **Locals visit for the lovely restaurant on-site** serving fresh Mediterranean fish and the dish Marseille is so famous for, Bouillabaisse. Here you'll eat family style on benches, sharing a table perhaps with locals. On-site boutique selling products of the land like olive oil, black truffle, and Bottarga. Amenities: Free Wi-Fi but here to need to bring your own toiletries.

Chapter 4
WHERE TO EAT

ALCYONE
INTERCONTINENTAL HOTEL DIEU
1 Place Daviel, Marseille, +33 4 13 42 43 43
www.ihg.com/intercontinental/hotels/gb/en/marseille/
mrsha/hoteldetail#eatanddrink
CUISINE: French
DRINKS: Full bar
SERVING: Lunch & Dinner; closed Sun
PRICE RANGE: $$$$
NEIGHBORHOOD: Minta Arah
Michelin Star awarded restaurant that offers an

innovative menu of seasonal dishes. The bouillabaisse here is a lot lighter than some of those you'll find elsewhere in town. Excellent French food served with a lighter touch. On game nights when the Olympique de Marseille soccer team plays, they open the terrace where they have a fun raucous grill night.

BAR DE LA MARINE
15, Quai de Rive Neuve, Marseille, 4-91-54-95-42
CUISINE: French, Mediterranean
DRINKS: Full Bar
SERVING: Breakfast & Lunch
PRICE RANGE: $$
NEIGHBORHOOD: Saint Victor
This famous Marseille institution is a popular spot for

breakfast and lunch. At night, however, it becomes a bar only, and it's just as much fun.

CHEZ FONFON
140, rue Vallon des Auffes, Marseille, 4-91-52-14-38
www.chezfonfon.com
CUISINE: Seafood
DRINKS: Full bar
SERVING: Lunch & Dinner
PRICE RANGE: $$$$
NEIGHBORHOOD: Endoume
Tucked away in a small inlet, Chez Fonfon has a wonderful view. In the summer, you can ride around the port in a boat. This is where you'll want to order the bouillabaisse. They're also famous for their roasted pigeon.

EPICERIE L'IDEAL

11 rue d'Aubagne, 13001 Marseille,
+33 9 80 39 99 41
www.epicerielideal.com
CUISINE: French/Deli
DRINKS: Beer & Wine
SERVING: Breakfast, Lunch, & Dinner; closed Sun & Mon
PRICE RANGE: $$
NEIGHBORHOOD: Noailles

Grocery store that offers a simple menu that changes daily. You'll find French and Italian gourmet goods bulging from the wooden shelves lining the walls. A few tables are available where you can eat. Busy all day with a loyal following. Meals prepared with fresh seasonal products. Vegetarian options. Nice selection of beers.

L'EPUISETTE

Vallon des Auffes, Marseille, +33 4 91 52 17 82
www.l-epuisette.fr/
CUISINE: French/Mediterranean
DRINKS: Full bar
SERVING: Lunch & Dinner; closed Sun & Mon
PRICE RANGE: $$$$
NEIGHBORHOOD: Endoume

There's been some sort of eatery on this spot—a rocky promontory jutting out into the sea beside a charming little fishing village—for over 50 years. From this vantage point you can see the Chateau d'If, an island fortress dating back to the 16th Century. What started out as nothing more than a little seafood shack has transformed into a light, modern restaurant decorated with travertine marble and light-colored woods. Great menu of French cuisine – try the tasting menu if you've never been here. The authentic Bouillabaisse here is served in 2 courses. First you get a deep brown bouillon made using bony rockfish and spiced with garlic and saffron. Next you'll get fillets of 5 different fish (monkfish, scorpion fish, gurnard, weever, John Dory), first stewed and then sauced at your table with more bouillon. There's a great appetizer of tuna with foi gras that's quite different from any version I've seen before. Extensive wine list representing all parts of Europe.

LA BOITE A SARDINE

2 boulevard de la Liberation, 13001 Marseille
+33 4 91 50 95 95
www.laboiteasardine.com
CUISINE: Seafood
DRINKS: Wine & Beer
SERVING: Breakfast/Lunch/Early Dinner
PRICE RANGE: $$$
NEIGHBORHOOD: Thier
Tiny restaurant offering a great selection of fresh seafood including lobster, chilled shrimp, raw, freshly shucked oysters and sea urchins. Menu changes daily because they have no written menu, just what seafood they are serving that day. Reservations recommended otherwise you can wait up to an hour. Note: they only speak French here.

LA CANTINETTA

24, Cours Julien F, Marseille, 33-4-91-48-10-48
https://www.facebook.com/pages/La-Cantinetta/153423988030261
CUISINE: Italian
DRINKS: Full Bar
SERVING: Lunch & Dinner
PRICE RANGE: $$
NEIGHBORHOOD: Notre Dame du Mont
No more French food for you? (If such a thing was possible.) Try this place for great Italian specialties. Big hams of prosciutto dangle from the ceiling. The mozzarella is made from cow's milk from Puglia.
I always get the superbly grilled veal chop when stopping in here, and in good weather, I always sit in the very nice garden out back.

LE BOUCHER

10 Rue de Village, 13006 Marseille,
+33 4 91 48 79 65
www.restaurant-leboucher.fr/restaurant-marseille

CUISINE: Steakhouse/French
DRINKS: Full bar
SERVING: Lunch & Dinner; closed Sun & Mon
PRICE RANGE: $$$
NEIGHBORHOOD: Castellane
Friendly steakhouse offering a simple menu with a French twist offering a variety of beef dishes but also European favorites like pig feet and lamb sweetbreads. Ideal for meat lovers. Nice wine selection. Reservations recommended.

LE MOLE PASSÉDAT

Prom. Pierre Laffont, Marseille, +33 4 91 19 17 80
www.passedat.fr/en
CUISINE: French/Mediterranean fusion
DRINKS: Full bar
SERVING: Lunch & Dinner; closed Sun
PRICE RANGE: $$$
NEIGHBORHOOD: La Joliette
This super chic modern restaurant is located on the top floor of the MUCEM museum where you'll really love the expansive terrace offering a great view. In fact, the view is probably the best one in the whole town—it overlooks the old port, the hills on top of which are perched ancient churches, and of course the Mediterranean Sea. There are choices here—a buffet on the terrace loaded with charcuterie items and great salads, seafood and cocktails. The other one is **La Table**, a much more upscale dining experience that requires reservations. Creative menu of dishes like: Octopus carpaccio; spelt risotto; pan-fried duck's liver; and crab meat with a lemony quinoa salad. The wine list emphasizes wines from Provence, as it should.

LE PETIT NICE PASSEDAT
17, rue des Braves, Marseille, 4-91-59-25-92
www.passedat.fr
CUISINE: French, Southwest
DRINKS: Full Bar
SERVING: Lunch & Dinner
PRICE RANGE: $$$$
NEIGHBORHOOD: Endoume

This expensive eatery is the city's only restaurant with
3 Michelin stars. Here, you'll want to focus on the
fish, fish, fish. Take the #83 bus from the Old Port and
disembark at Anse de la Fausse Monnaie. Go down
to the harbor and you'll be there. Well worth the high
prices.

LE VENTRE DE L'ARCHITECTE
280, Blvd Michelet, Marseille, 4-9-16-78-23
www.hotellecorbusier.com/restaurant/
CUISINE: French
DRINKS: Full Bar
SERVING: Lunch & Dinner
PRICE RANGE: $$$$
NEIGHBORHOOD: Bompard
There are some Asian influences in this cuisine. Very
expensive, but it's quite a show. (The views are really
excellent.)

LES ARCENAULX

25, cours Honoré d'Estienne d'Orves, Marseilles,
4-91-59-80-30

www.les-arcenaulx.com

CUISINE: French, Regional

DRINKS: Full Bar

SERVING: Lunch & Dinner

PRICE RANGE: $$$$

This is a 30 year old landmark. While the walls are
lined with books like a library, you won't want to
bury your nose in a book while you're here. You can
expect a delectable culinary experience such as the
scallops on a bed of sweet potato galette. Refined
cuisine in a pleasant atmosphere. Enjoy the desserts
as well with a great selection of teas in the afternoon.
Excellent service.

MIRAMAR

12, quai du Port, Marseilles, 4-91-91-10-40
www.lemiramar.fr
CUISINE: French, Regional Southwestern
DRINKS: Full Bar
SERVING: Lunch & Dinner
PRICE RANGE: $$$$

The concierge at my hotel gave me several recommendations for dining. This was one of them and I wasn't disappointed. The Bouillabaisse here is for two persons, delivered tableside, beautifully presented. Infused with "Ricard." It has a distinctive flavor. Incredible fish soup. Very pricey but the quality is all here.

PÉRON

56 Promenade de la Corniche John Kennedy,
Marseille, +33 4 91 52 15 22
www.restaurant-peron.com
CUISINE: Modern European/Seafood
DRINKS: Full bar
SERVING: Lunch & Dinner
PRICE RANGE: $$$$
NEIGHBORHOOD: Endoume

Great upscale French eatery (food is as good as that at
Le Petit Nice, but not as expensive) that fills up with
locals – first seating at 8 p.m. is recommended before
it gets busy. Expect a traditional 7 course French
dinner. Extensive wine list. Great views overlooking
the Mediterranean Sea. Delicious desserts – order
early as they run out.

SOUS LES MICOCOULIERS

13810 Traverse Montfort, Eygalières, +04 90 95 94 53
www.souslesmicocouliers.com
CUISINE: French/Provencal
DRINKS: Full bar
SERVING: Lunch & Dinner
PRICE RANGE: $$$
NEIGHBORHOOD: Traverse Montfort

Chef Pierre Louis Poize offers a gourmet menu focusing on local and seasonal ingredients. The restaurant features indoor and outdoor dining – check out the beautiful courtyard with 200 year-old trees. Menu picks: Lobster grilled with chestnuts and Carpachio Salmon. Nice wine list.

TOINOU

3 cours Saint-Louis, Marseille, + 04 91 33 14 94
www.toinou.com
CUISINE: Seafood/Market
DRINKS: No Booze
SERVING: Open daily
PRICE RANGE: $$
NEIGHBORHOOD: Noailles
This famous Marseille spot has been around since the 1960s, and has ever since then specialized in offering shellfish caught along the cost, like oysters from the Carmargue and mussels from Bouzigues in the south of France. Nice selection of plates of oysters, lobster, other succulent shellfish and a fish of the day. Open 7 days. Delivery available.

VILLA MARIE JEANNE

4 Rue Chicot, Marseille, +33 4 91 85 51 31
www.villa-marie-jeanne.com
NEIGHBORHOOD: Saint Barnabé
An 18th century stone manor house transformed into a wonderful Bed & Breakfast that offers 3 charming rooms, and 2 apartments. **Locals visit for the lovely restaurant on-site** serving fresh Mediterranean fish and the dish Marseille is so famous for, Bouillabaisse. Here you'll eat family style on benches, sharing a table perhaps with locals. On-site boutique selling

products of the land like olive oil, black truffle, and Bottarga. Amenities: Free Wi-Fi but here to need to bring your own toiletries.

Chapter 5
NIGHTLIFE

AU PETIT NICE
28, Place Jean Jaures, Marseille, 4-91-48-43-04
NEIGHBORHOOD: Le Camas; La Plaine
No Website
Nice bar in trendy La Plaine.

LA DAME NOIRE
43, Quai de Rive Neuve, Marseille, +33 4 91 66 61 37
NEIGHBORHOOD: Notre Dame du Mont
No Website
The lights are low in this sexy lounge. Top place in
town for DJs spinning electronica. Till 6 a.m.

LE CARRE
36, Blvd Charles Livon, Marseille, 4-91-15-59-60
NEIGHBORHOOD: Le Pharo
www.sofitel-marseille-vieuxport.com
Here in the lobby of the **Sofitel Vieux Port** is a lovely
lounge with lots of specialty cocktails to go with the
killer view of the Vieux Port.

VICTOR CAFÉ
71, Blvd Charles Livon, Marseille, 4-88-00-46-00
NEIGHBORHOOD: Le Pharo
www.victorcafemarseille.com
Inside the color is pink, which matches well with
the outdoor pool glowing green. Superbly executed
cocktails.

Chapter 6
WHAT TO SEE & DO

CENTRE DE LA VIEILLE CHARITE
2, rue de la Charite, Marseille, 4-91-14-58-80
NEIGHBORHOOD: Les Grandes Carmes
www.vieille-charite-marseille.com/
This used to be an almshouse, but it has been
creatively turned into a great museum, or really, a
series of museums and arts institutions. In 1640,
following the royal edict on "confinement of the
poor and beggars," the City of Marseille, the owner
of land located on the northern slope of the hills,

decided to build the Old Charity to accommodate the beggars. But the project stalled and it was only in 1670 that Pierre Puget, the king's architect who was from the area, began one of his greatest achievements. It's been going ever since. This charming neighborhood makes for a good stroll. What used to be a home for sailors, immigrants and the poor, with its cobbled streets and colorfully painted houses, now is home to artisans and professional people.

CROISIERES MARSEILLE CALANQUES

1 Canebière, Marseille, 4-91-58-50-58
NEIGHBORHOOD: Opera
www.croisieres-marseille-calanques.com
A variety of tours available here. Don't forget that Marseille was settled by the Greeks around 600 BC. To get a good idea what the sometimes unforgiving rugged coast looks like, take one of these cheap hour-long boat tours. You'll want to see the "Calanques," the series of stunning limestone cliffs and coves

stretching between Marseille and Cassis. (These were recently named the newest national park in France.) On either side of the port you'll see from the water the 2 forts dating back to the 17th Century: St.-Jean (actually goes back to the 12th Century) and St.-Nicolas. Another treat is the **Cathédrale de la Major**, designed in the Byzantine style, as well as the **Île d'If** and its fort, the **Château d'If**. This 16th Century fortress was later turned into a prison made famous by Dumas in **"The Count of Monte Cristo."**

LA BASTIDE DES BAINS
19, rue Sainte, Marseille, 4-91-33-39-13
NEIGHBORHOOD: Opera
www.bastide-des-bains.com
Traditional hammam (Turkish bath) housed in an old printing house.

LA CORNICHE
This is the famous boulevard that hugs the
Mediterranean that you'll want to walk up and down
as you take in the sights and inhale the salty air.

LA S JULIEN
Cours Julien, Marseille, No Phone
NEIGHBORHOOD: Notre Dame du Mont
www.coursjulien.marsnet.org
WEBSITE DOWN AT PRESSTIME
Scenic courtyard that draws the young and hip.
Lots of places to hang out, with bars and cafes and
boutiques everywhere.

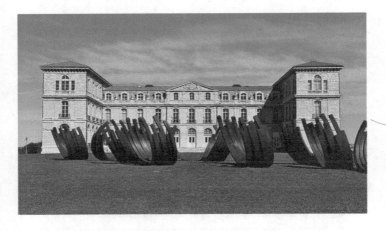

LE PALAIS DU PHARO
58, Blvd Charles Livon, Marseille, 4-91-14-64-95
NEIGHBORHOOD: Le Pharo
http://palaisdupharo.marseille.fr
You can sit on the lawn at **Napoleon III's Palace** by
the sea to look at the great view and the other people
looking at it with you.

MUSEE D'ART CONTEMPORAIN MAC
69, Ave de Haifa, Marseille, 4-91-25-01-07
NEIGHBORHOOD: Sainte Anne
www.lesartistescontemporains.com/macmarseille.html
The late César Baldaccini was the most renowned
of local arts champions. This museum is crammed
with his neo-realist sculptures. Like the compacted
autos that always attract curious stares. Many other
artists represented, such as Jean-Michel Basquiat and
Dieter Roth.

MuCEM
MUSÉE DES CIVILISATIONS DE L'EUROPE
ET DE LA MÉDITERRANÉE
MUSEUM OF EUROPEAN &
MEDITERRANEAN CIVILIZATIONS
Right on the edge of the port of Marseille is this
spectacular museum that opened in 2016. Not only
does it have stunning views of the harbor and the sea,
but the architecture is eye opening as well. Its

historical collections are superior and their exhibitions cover not only European but North African cultures as well, recognizing the importance over the centuries that Africa has played in the growth and development of Marseille. The job of putting this all together fell to architect Rudy Ricciotti, who worked hard to combine the new building with the 17th Century Fort St.-Jean, connecting it using foot bridges to the modernist glass structure. The outdoor skin covering the top of the building represents a fishing net, so perfect for Marseille, right?

NOTRE-DAME-DU-MONT
This neighborhood is close to three metro stations. It is a short walk to the Old Port, popular for its bars and restaurants and for the Notre-Dame Church atop a hill that towers above it all.

Chapter 7
SHOPPING & SERVICES

You will definitely want to check out the **Cours Julien** district—this is where you'll find lots of interesting shops.

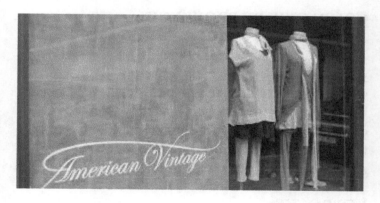

31 Rue Francis Davso, Marseille, 4-91-33-43-46
www.americanvintage-store.com/fr
An empty suitcase could be useful as you hit Rue Sainte, where local fashion labels have sprouted up. Though the name is misleading — the brand is Marseille-based and sells new threads — the subdued colors and ultrathin fabrics have garnered enough fans to generate boutiques from Amsterdam to Tel Aviv.

COMPAGNIE DE PROVENCE
18, rue Davso, 33-4-91-33-04-17
1, rue Crates, Marseille, 4-91-56-20-94
www.compagniedeprovence.com
Olive and vegetable based soaps. They have 2 shops
here in town. I once got some lavender scented
exfoliating soap in this shop and use it to this day.
(I still order from them, only now I do it through
Amazon.) Really great soaps.

LES DOCKS
10 Place de la Joliette, Marseille.
http://www.lesdocks-marseille.com/en/
NEIGHBORHOOD: La Joliette
This unique complex is a recently opened city center
that houses over 200 companies, situated in a series
of cargo warehouses and terminals that make the port
even more pedestrian friendly than it was before.
Approximately 60 shopping outlets, local restaurants,
service providers and artisans. Open daily.

LES HALLES DE LA MAJOR

Les Voûtes de la Major, 12 Quai de la Tourette, Marseille, +33 4 91 45 80 10

www.leshallesdelamajor.com/en/

NEIGHBORHOOD: **La Joliette**

By day a farmer's market and food hall featuring great selections of gourmet foods, sandwiches, seafood, and local cuisine. Open seating at picnic tables, ultra casual. A great selection of different foods—try to veal tartare at **La Boucherie**, or the excellent mint fritters or the delectable fried zucchini rom **Las Tapas des Halles**. From **La Poissonnerie**, you can refresh yourself with a plate for salty oysters. At night the place is transformed into a gathering place and venue for special events and entertainment.

OOGIE

55, Cours Julien, Marseille, 4-91-53-10-70

NEIGHBORHOOD: Notre Dame du Mont

www.oogie.eu

A concept store with its own café and hair salon in the La Plaine district. Men's and women's clothing, accessories.

SESSUN
6, rue Sainte, Marseilles, 4-91-52-33-61
NEIGHBORHOOD: Vauban
www.sessun.com
The colors and design get more adventurous at,
where you can pick up funky hot pants with a graph-
paper motif.

ZEIN ORIENTAL SPA

16, Quai Rive Neuve, Marseille, 4-91-59-11-11
https://marseille.zeinorientalspa.fr
NEIGHBORHOOD: Saint Victor
Tucked in an alley along the Vieux Port, an upscale
hammam-spa that opened last year, is very 1,001
Nights with its keyhole doorways, Moorish tilework,
spice-scented air and soft Arabo-electro music. The
Hammam Jasmin package includes a rubdown in
olive-oil soap, an exfoliation by an attendant with a
rough glove, and a half-hour massage.

INDEX

Other Books by the Same Author

Andrew Delaplaine has written in widely varied fields: screenplays, novels (adult and juvenile), travel writing, journalism. His books are available in quality bookstores as well as all online retailers.

JACK HOUSTON / ST. CLAIR POLITICAL THRILLERS

THE KEYSTONE FILE – PART 1 - 7

On Election night, as China and Russia mass soldiers on their common border in preparation for war, there's a tie in the Electoral College that forces the decision for President into the House of Representatives as mandated by the Constitution. The incumbent Republican President, working through his Aide for Congressional Liaison, uses the Keystone File, which contains dirt on every member of Congress, to blackmail members into supporting the Republican candidate. The action runs from Election Night in November to Inauguration Day on January 20. Jack Houston St. Clair runs a small detective agency in Miami. His father is Florida Governor Sam Houston St. Clair, the Republican candidate. While he tries to help his dad win the election, Jack also gets hired to follow up on some

suspicious wire transfers involving drug smugglers, leading him to a sunken narco-sub off Key West that has $65 million in cash in its hull.

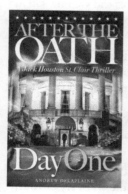
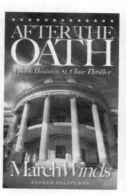

AFTER THE OATH: DAY ONE
AFTER THE OATH: MARCH WINDS
WEDDING AT THE WHITE HOUSE

Only three months have passed since Sam Houston St. Clair was sworn in as the new President, but a lot has happened. Returning from Vienna where he met with Russian and Chinese diplomats, Sam is making his way back to Flagler Hall in Miami, his first trip home since being inaugurated. Son Jack is in the midst of turmoil of his own back in Miami, dealing with various dramas, not the least of which is his increasing alienation from Babylon Fuentes and his growing attraction to the seductive Lupe Rodriguez. Fernando Pozo addresses new problems as he struggles to expand Cuba's secret operations in the U.S., made even more difficult as U.S.-Cuban relations thaw. As his father returns home, Jack knows Sam will find as much trouble at home as he did in Vienna.

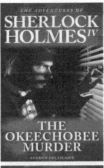

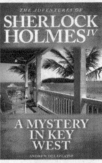

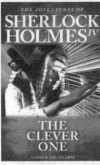

THE ADVENTURES OF SHERLOCK HOLMES IV

In this series, the original Sherlock Holmes's great-great-great grandson solves crimes and mysteries in the present day, working out of the boutique whotel he owns on South Beach.

THE OKEECHOBEE MURDER

Sherlock Holmes and Watson are called to a remote area of Florida overlooking Lake Okeechobee to investigate a murder where all the evidence points to the victim's son as the killer. Holmes, however, is not so sure.

A MYSTERY IN KEY WEST

Holmes's doctor orders him to take a short holiday in Key West, and while there, Holmes is called on to look into a case in which three people involved in a Santería ritual died with no explanation.

THE CLEVER ONE

A former nun who, while still very devout, has renounced her vows so that she could "find a life, and possibly love, in the real world." She comes to Holmes in hopes that he can find out what happened to the man who promised to marry her, but mysteriously disappeared moments before their wedding.

ENIGMA IN THE REDLANDS

A nanny reaches out to Sherlock Holmes seeking his advice on whether she should take a new position when her prospective employer has demanded that she cut her hair as part of the job.

THE ADVENTURES OF SHERLOCK HOLMES IV

In this series, the original Sherlock Holmes's great-great-great grandson solves crimes and mysteries in the present day, working out of the boutique whotel he owns on South Beach.

THE RED-HAIRED MAN
A man with a shock of red hair calls on Sherlock Holmes to solve the mystery of the Red-haired League.

TOO MANY NAPOLEONS
Inspector Lestrade calls on Holmes to help him figure out why a madman would go around Miami breaking into homes and businesses to destroy cheap busts of the French Emperor. It all seems very insignificant to Holmes—until, of course, a murder occurs.

THE MISSING MAN IN THE WINDOW
In what seems to be the case of a missing person, Sherlock Holmes navigates his way through a maze of perplexing clues that leads him through a sinister world to a surprising conclusion.

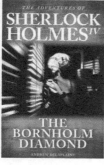

THE BORNHOLM DIAMOND
A mysterious Swedish nobleman requests a meeting to discuss a matter of such serious importance that it may threaten the line of succession in one of the oldest royal houses in Europe.

THE MIDNIGHT MASS SERIES – AN AMOS FREEMAN THRILLER

MIDNIGHT MASS: THE CRIME
MIDNIGHT MASS: THE INVESTIGATION
MIDNIGHT MASS: THE BREAK
MIDNIGHT MASS: THE CHASE

It's Christmas Eve in New York. Men in hooded monks' robes and plastic masks of the face of Jesus Christ have just pulled off a spectacular robbery of the oldest church in town, getting away with tens of millions of dollars in jewelry and cash and also killing fifteen of the congregation.

Stumbling onto the scene is Lieutenant Amos Freeman, on his way home to Brooklyn after buying presents for the wife he no longer loves, and after stopping by his favorite haunt, Big Dot's Jungle Bar, for a few drinks (or as Big Dot often says, "a few too many").

Freeman snaps into professional mode, quickly assuming command of a chaotic situation, and in the process, making a big impression on a furious Mayor Frederick Lindstadt, who had been mocked and humiliated by the robbers for being not only short and bald, but helpless as well.

When the TV crews bear down and police brass arrive to take charge, Amos Freeman, not a big fan of police department politics, melts into the background, but not for long.

THE DELAPLAINE LONG WEEKEND TRAVEL GUIDE SERIES

Delaplaine Travel Guides represent the author's take on some of the many cities he's visited and many of which he has called home (for months or even years) during a lifetime of travel. The books are available as either ebooks or as printed books. Owing to the ease with which material can be uploaded, both the printed and ebook editions are updated 3 times a year.

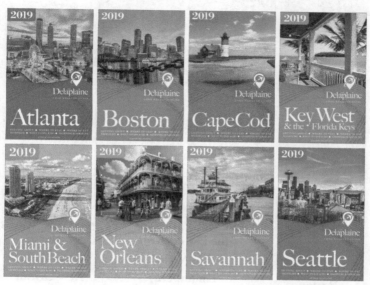

Atlanta

Austin

Boston

Cancún (Mexico)

Cannes

Cape Cod

Charleston

Chicago

Clearwater – St. Petersburg

Fort Lauderdale

Fort Myers & Sanibel

Gettysburg

Hamptons, The

Key West & the Florida Keys

Las Vegas

Louisville

Marseille

Martha's Vineyard

Memphis

Mérida (Mexico)

Mexico City

Miami & South Beach

Milwaukee

Myrtle Beach

Nantucket

Napa Valley

Naples & Marco Island

Nashville

New Orleans

Newport (R.I.)

Philadelphia

Provincetown

Savannah

Seattle

THE FOOD ENTHUSIAST'S COMPLETE RESTAURANT GUIDES

Atlanta
Austin
Barcelona
Boston
Brooklyn
Buenos Aires
Cannes
Cape Cod
Charleston
Chicago
Florence
Fort Lauderdale
Fort Myers & Sanibel
Gettysburg
Hampton, The

Key West & the Florida Keys
Las Vegas
Lima (Peru)
London
Los Angeles
Louisville
Marseille
Martha's Vineyard
Memphis
Mérida (Mexico)
Mexico City
Miami & South Beach
Milwaukee
Napa Valley

Naples & Marco Island
Nashville
New Orleans
Newport (R.I.)
New York / Manhattan
Paris
Philadelphia
Portland (Ore.)
Provincetown
San Diego
San Juan
Savannah
Seattle
Tampa Bay